MYSTERIOUS PYRAMIDS

Qin Mausoleum: *Tomb of China's First Emperor*

Murray "Oak" Tapeta

A Crabtree Crown Book

Crabtree Publishing

crabtreebooks.com

Teaching Tips for Caregivers:

You can help your child learn by encouraging them to read widely, both as a leisure activity and as a way of satisfying their curiosity about the world. Reading helps build a strong foundation in language and literacy skills that will help your child succeed in school. This high-interest book will appeal to all readers in intermediate and middle school grades.

Use the following suggestions to help your child grow as a reader.

- Encourage them to read independently at home.
- Encourage them to practice reading aloud.
- Encourage activities that require reading.
- Establish a regular reading time.
- Have your child ask and answer questions about what they read.

Teaching Tips for Teachers:

Engage students throughout the reading process by asking questions like these.

Before Reading

- Ask, "What do you already know about this topic?"
- Ask, "What do you want to learn about this topic?"

During Reading

- Ask, "What is the author trying to teach you?"
- Ask, "How is this like something you have read or seen before?"
- Ask, "How do the text features (headings, index, etc.) help you understand the topic?"

After Reading

- Ask, "What interesting or fun fact did you learn about Qin Shi Huang or his mausoleum?"
- Ask, "What questions do you still have about the Qin mausoleum? How could you find the answers?"

TABLE OF CONTENTS

A PUZZLE FROM THE PAST

The world is full of mysterious places that hold the secrets of lost civilizations. Ancient ruins are like snapshots in time. They provide us with important clues about what life was like long, long ago.

Pyramids usually served as grand burial chambers for royalty or as temples for religious ceremonies or both. These structures exist in various forms around the world, built by civilizations that had little or no contact with one another.

The **mausoleum**, or burial place, of the first Emperor of China was a pyramid buried underground! Soil was mounded on top, and trees were planted so that the site looks like a low, wooded mountain.

PYRAMID STYLES

Giza - True pyramid

Teotihuacán - Talud-tablero pyramid

China's first emperor Qin Shi Huang had his tomb built in the shape of a **truncated** pyramid. This style of pyramid does not rise to a point and appears cut off at the top. To protect against **looting** of its treasures, the pyramid was buried and made to look like a hill. This human-made burial mound is called a **tumulus**.

Emperor Qin wanted an entire underground kingdom built around his tomb. Construction on the massive mausoleum went on for nearly 40 years. In 210 BCE, the emperor died.

Borobudur - Step pyramid

Ziggurat of Ur - Step pyramid

2600 BCE — **Giza**

2500 BCE

2100 BCE — **Ziggurat of Ur** — **2000 BCE**

900 BCE — **Tikal**

259 BCE — **Qin Emperor**

Qin Emperor - Buried flat-topped, step pyramid

Tikal - Step pyramid

BUILT TO IMPRESS!

Why did so many different ancient cultures build similar towering shapes? Relying on the forces of nature, ancient builders learned that the taller you build, the bigger you had to make the base. This helped distribute the weight more toward the bottom so a very tall structure would not topple over.

210 BCE

100 CE

Teotihuacán

450 CE

778 CE

Borobudur

850 CE

900 CE

China
QIN MAUSOLEUM
East
China
Sea
South China
Sea

THE FIRST EMPEROR

In ancient times, China was made up of many warring kingdoms. Qin Shi Huang became king of the powerful state of Qin in 246 BCE when he was just 13 years old. Under his leadership, the kingdom of Qin defeated six other states and joined them together under one ruler for the first time. Ending hundreds of years of bloodshed, Qin declared himself China's first emperor in 221 BCE. A unified China took its name from the state of Qin, pronounced "chin."

Although the Qin dynasty was brief (221–207 BCE), the achievements during that period were significant and long-lasting. All the different kingdoms now followed the same laws, writing, money, weights, and measurements. Along with building a network of roads and canals, Qin Shi Huang began connecting defensive walls and fortresses together to defend the empire against invaders. The massive **fortification** would become what we know today as the Great Wall of China.

Statue of Emperor Qin Shi Huang

The Great Wall has been called the longest graveyard in the world. Thousands of workers died building the wall—about one for every 5 feet (1.5 m) of wall built! The wall was completed over hundreds of years from the 5th century BCE to 16th century CE.

A FARMER'S FIND

In March 1974, a farmer named Yang Zhifa was digging a well outside the city of Xi'an, China. Other farmers helped him. After three days, they uncovered a surprise. Buried in the soil were solid arms, legs, heads, and torsos. The body parts were made of **terra-cotta**. They seemed to be pieces of life-sized statues. Digging a little deeper, they found more clay statues as well as bronze **artifacts**. The farmers alerted a museum, and **archaeologists** took over the dig. Soon, they discovered underground vaults. Inside were thousands of statues of soldiers made of terra-cotta. They stood silently in columns as if ready for battle.

A Silent Army

Archaeologists believe Qin was buried with more than 8,000 terra-cotta soldiers. Each clay warrior is unique. The statues have different postures, facial expressions, physical features, clothing, and hairstyles. When the warriors were created, they were painted in different colors. Unfortunately, the layers of paint flaked away as they were dug up, leaving just the brown clay.

AN EMPEROR'S ETERNAL EMPIRE

The farmers had discovered something incredible. The chamber they unearthed was only one small part of the massive tomb complex of Emperor Qin Shi Huang. The emperor's actual burial place was built inside a large four-sided, truncated pyramid. The pyramid is only part of a huge compound that stretches for more than 20 square miles (60 square kilometers). The terra-cotta soldiers were found nearly a mile (1.5 kilometers) away from the pyramid.

Qin had workers begin work on his tomb during his reign. Historians estimate that it took over 700,000 people to build the enormous complex. Construction on the massive mausoleum went on for nearly 40 years. It is believed that skilled craftspeople worked alongside prisoners. The city of Liyi was constructed near the complex so that workers would have some place to live. Many human skeletons have been discovered at the complex. It is believed that after workers placed objects in the vaults, they, too, were sealed inside and left to die to keep the tomb's location secret.

Sima Qian, an ancient Chinese historian, wrote a very detailed description of the construction of the tomb and the enormous complex it was part of. As the centuries passed, the location of the emperor's tomb was not forgotten. But Sima Qian's account of the grand underground city built around it began to be thought of as more legend than fact.

The vast underground complex has many parts. An outer wall surrounds the area. Inner walls stand inside. Buildings include palaces, offices, and horse stables. There are also many smaller tombs. Experts believe that the entire layout resembles Xianyang, the capital city of the Qin empire.

About 600 pits, or vaults, lay underneath the site. Some contain the Terra-cotta Army. Perhaps the most amazing finds in the tomb of Emperor Qin Shi Huang were two bronze **chariots**. They are pulled by four bronze horses decorated with gold and silver. The horses' job was to transport the emperor in the **afterlife**.

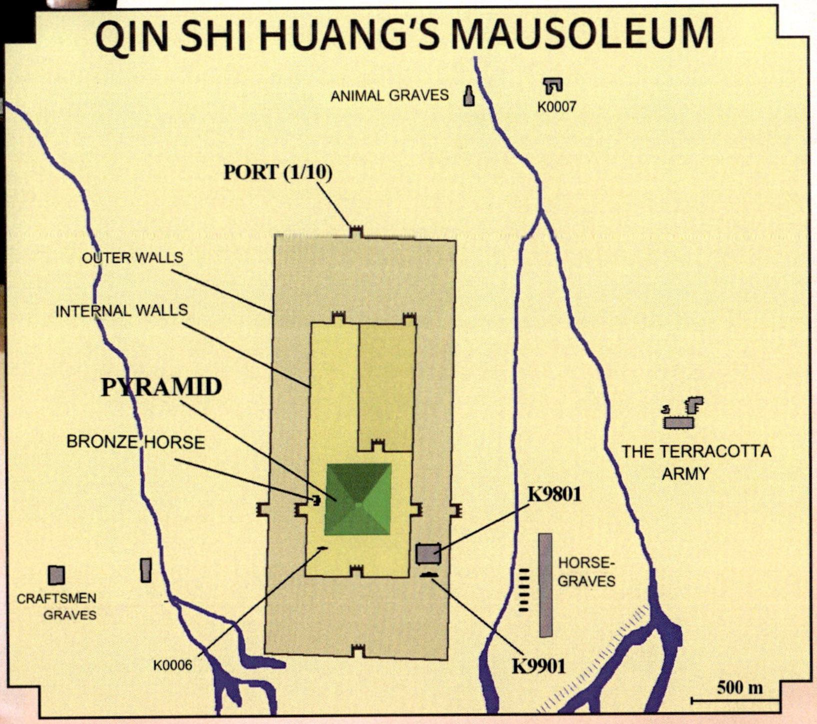

DO NOT DISTURB

Originally as high as 377 feet (115 meters), the tumulus, or burial hill, rises about 168 feet (51 meters) high today. The tomb's pyramid lies at the center of the complex. Emperor Qin's mausoleum is inside. Historian Sima Qian's ancient writings say that it would be dangerous to disturb it. He warned that traps are set for any robbers who dare to come near the grave. They include real crossbows that will automatically fire arrows. A river of **mercury** is said to surround the tomb. In 2020, scientists tested the site to see if the old claims were true. The results did show higher than normal levels of mercury in the area. The chemical is toxic to humans.

Qin's tomb itself has not yet been **excavated** for fear of damaging the heritage site and its contents. Seeing the damage done to the unearthed terra-cotta figures, archaeologists worry that they may not yet have good techniques for preserving any precious objects they find inside. The safety of workers is also a concern due to the high levels of mercury in the ground. There is also another important reason for leaving the burial place unexplored. The Chinese people want to respect the resting place of their ancient emperor.

IMMORTAL KING

One of Emperor Qin Shi Huang's keenest interests was finding a way to live forever. One theory was that his physicians suggested he drink mercury. It is not known yet what his actual cause of death was, but records show he lived to the age of 49.

UNDERGROUND TREASURES

Archaeologists have been working on the site since 1974, when the Terra-cotta Army was discovered. Only a small percentage of the area has been excavated. It is a slow, careful process. No one wants to damage the priceless artifacts. Over 2,000 terra-cotta warriors have been found. Archaeologists think that 6,000 more may remain buried. The soldiers are arranged in battle formation. They face east, the direction from which Emperor Qin's enemies might approach.

Some of the warriors carry bronze swords, spears, and crossbows. The weapons are still shiny and sharp. The vaults also contained bronze chariots and bronze horses with leather bridles. In keeping with the tradition of kings, the emperor was also buried with real horses. In fact, hundreds of sacrificed horses were found in the stables along with terra-cotta attendants to care for them.

Excavation was stopped until scientists figured out a way to prevent paint from flaking off the terra-cotta statues when they were exposed to the air.

Bronze Chariot

AFTERLIFE

The ancient Chinese believed in a life after death, called the afterlife. Most people on their journey after death were buried with things they might need, such as food, clothes, and jewelry. Qin Shi Huang was no different. But the necessities of a king are on a much grander scale. In addition to his Terra-cotta Army, archaeologists found iron tools and decorative objects made of silk, linen, **jade**, and bone.

Having servants during his lifetime, the emperor would also need servants in his afterlife. Terra-cotta statues of servants, workers, administrators, and even entertainers populated Qin's underground city. Many tombs and bodies have been found within the complex. A mass grave has also been found with the bones of young women. The women were likely the emperor's **concubines**.

AN ANCIENT ZOO

While animals were usually used for work in ancient China, there is evidence some species were kept in a kind of zoo, simply to be admired. One pit in Qin's mausoleum contained the remains of cranes, swans, and muntjacs, which are deer with small tusks.

SCIENCE SOLVES IT

Archaeologists and scientists have been using modern technologies to look before they dig and preserve what they find. Ground-penetrating radar can see Qin's underground vault. Although it is buried, archaeologists know where the tomb is and that the brick walls surrounding it are 45 feet tall, 410 feet wide, and 476 feet long (14 meters tall, 125 meters wide, and 145 meters long). Underneath the walls is a sort of upside-down pyramid. Qin's burial chamber is at the bottom point. They can also tell there are high mercury levels underground by testing core samples of the burial hill.

Weapons found with the Terracotta Army are tested with special X-ray scanners. That way they can determine the metals and chemicals contained in them without causing damage to them. Digital images taken of skulls and bones found in the site's cemeteries and pits are used to create computer models of what these people looked like.

WRAP IT UP

Sometimes the simplest solution is the best. Because of the type of paints used on the terra-cotta figures, they quickly become covered in **mold** when they are exposed to the air. Thanks to **forensic** science, archaeologists have developed ways to preserve the figures. They are now sprayed with an **antifungal** liquid and quickly wrapped in plastic wrap!

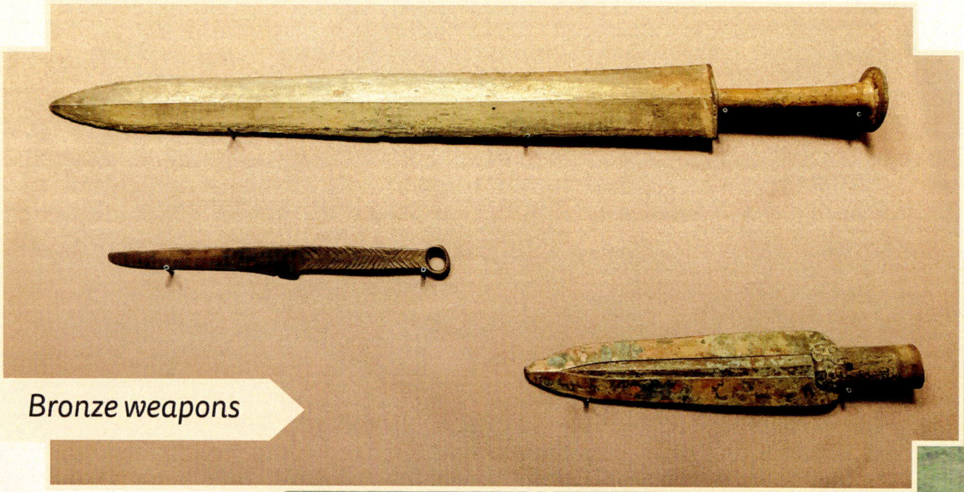

Bronze weapons

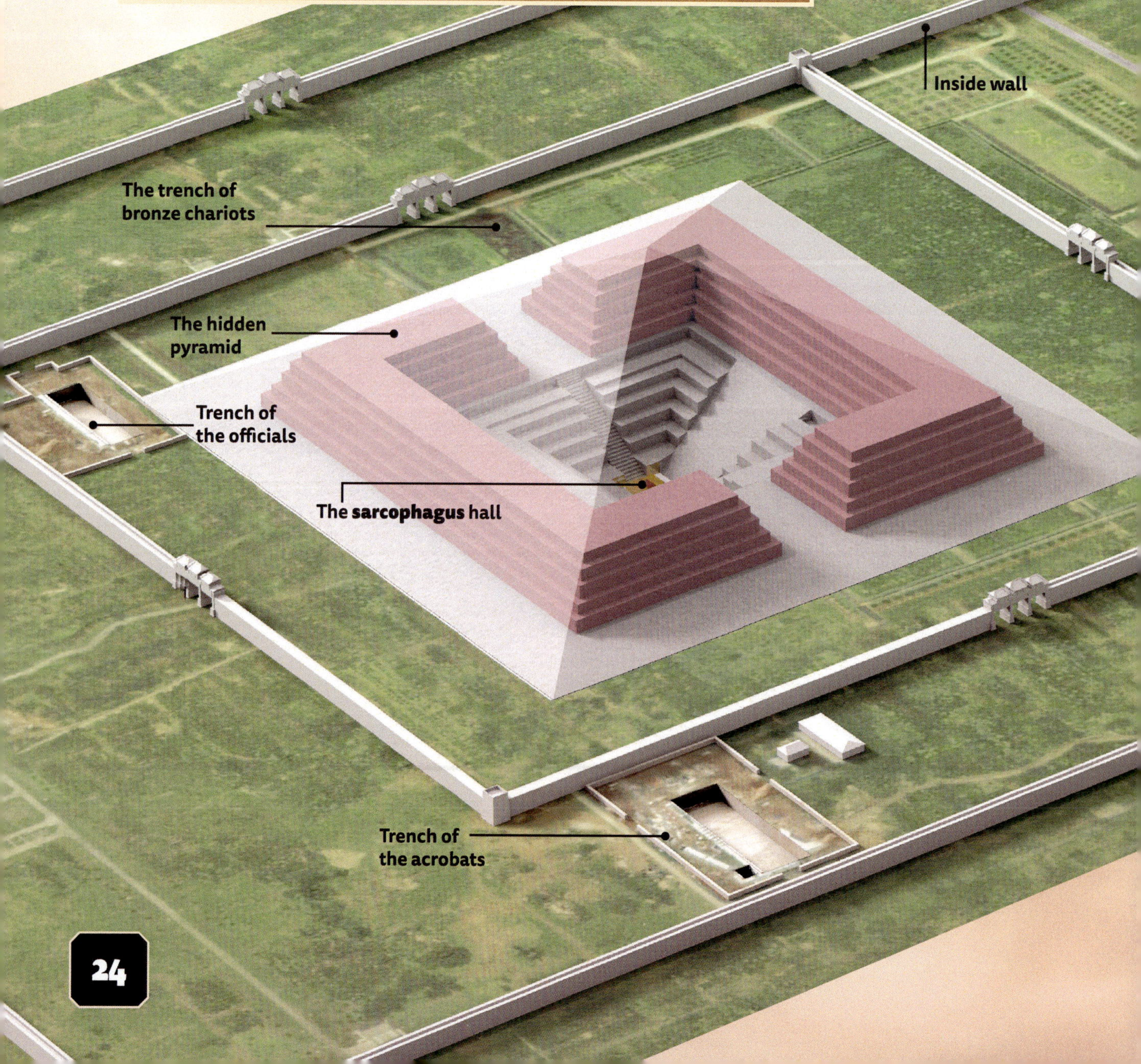

STOLEN HISTORY

The most valuable items may remain hidden in Emperor Qin's tomb inside the pyramid. Sima Qian wrote that the burial chamber was decorated with precious stones and metals. There were birds made of gold and silver and trees made of jade. Overhead, pearls were arranged to look like **constellations** in the night sky. Lamps were filled with whale oil that would burn for many years. We may never know if these details are true.

For centuries, many of China's ancient artifacts have been taken out of the country and held in museums in other countries. Some were sold and some were stolen. China is attempting to have all of these important **relics** returned. Sima Qian's historical record suggests Qin's mausoleum was looted and burned after the Qin dynasty fell. There is evidence of some damage to the other tombs in the complex, but archaeologists think it's possible Qin's tomb is still sealed and intact.

Wine vessel

A SITE TO SEE

You can visit the site to see the amazing Terra-cotta Army for yourself. The vaults are covered by an enormous building that looks like an airplane hangar. There, you can witness thousands of the amazingly detailed statues. They are eternally standing guard for their emperor who died more than two thousand years ago.

Archaeologists continue to explore the huge compound. They use traditional excavation methods as well as remote-sensing technology that allows them to map underground objects. They're discovering more clues that help tell the story of the mysterious pyramid and the powerful emperor who still rules his silent, underground kingdom.

In 1987, the Mausoleum of the First Qin Emperor was added to the UNESCO World Heritage List. This organization works to protect unique historical and cultural sites considered important to the entire world. To minimize threats to the site from urban development and tourism, China's Shaanxi provincial government also approved the *Conservation Plan for Qinshihuang Mausoleum* in July 2010. It sets boundaries around the site that the nearby district of Lintong cannot be developed beyond.

Emperor Qin Shi Huang

Primarily rural before the discovery nearby of the Terra-cotta Army, the county of Lintong grew quickly to become a major tourist center. Its rapid development threatens to encroach on the historic site.

GLOSSARY

afterlife (AF-ter-lyfe) Life that is believed to begin after death

antifungal (an-tee-FUN-gul) Used to prevent the growth of fungus

archaeologists (ahr-kee-AH-luh-juhsts) Scientists who study the distant past by digging up things that people made, used, and left behind

artifacts (AHR-tuh-fakts) Objects made and used by humans in the past, including tools and weapons

chariots (CHAR-ee-uhts) Light, horse-drawn carriages with two or four wheels that were often used in ancient times during battles and races

civilizations (siv-uh-li-ZAY-shuhnz) Groups of people with their own language and way of life

concubines (KON-kyuh-bynz) Unmarried women who served in the emperor's household as secondary wives but who held a lower status than his wife or wives

constellations (KON-stuh-LAY-shunz) Groups of stars that look like specific shapes or patterns and have been given names

excavated (EK-skuh-vay-tuhd) Found by digging in the soil

forensic (fuh-REN-sik) Relating to scientific tests or methods used when investigating crime

fortification (fawr-tuh-fuh-KAY-shuhn) A wall or strong structure built to protect against an attack

jade (jade) A hard, blue-green stone used for making jewelry and ornaments

looting (loo-ting) Forcefully taking goods or stealing

mausoleum (maw-zuh-LEE-uhm) A building that contains a tomb

mercury (MUR-kyur-ee) A silvery metal that is poisonous and liquid at room temperature

relics (REL-iks) Objects from an earlier time that have sentimental or historical importance

sarcophagus (sahr-KAH-fuh-guhs) A stone coffin

terra-cotta (TER-uh KAH-tuh) A hard, waterproof clay that is baked to make pottery, roof tiles, and other objects

truncated (trung-KAY-tuhd) Without an end or top section

tumulus (TOO-myuh-luhs) A mound of earth over top of a grave

INDEX

QUESTIONS AFTER READING

1. Emperor Qin's tomb is said to be surrounded by a river of _____.
   a. water
   b. mercury
   c. bronze
2. Archaeologists have known about the Terra-cotta Army ______.
   a. for 40 years
   b. since 1974
   c. since 246 BCE
3. Which of the following is not true of the terra-cotta warriors?
   a. They face west.
   b. They were once painted with bright colors.
   c. Each one has a unique look.
4. Emperor Qin wanted ____.
   a. to be found after his death
   b. to divide China into different parts
   c. to live forever
5. One reason Emperor Qin's tomb has not been excavated is ______.
   a. because archaeologists don't know where it is
   b. because it is cursed
   c. because it is believed to contain high levels of mercury

Answers: 1. b, 2. b, 3. a, 4. c, 5. c

ABOUT THE AUTHOR

Murray "Oak" Tapeta was born in a toilet-less cabin in Montana. Growing up in the great outdoors, he learned to love trees. He got the nickname "Oak" after climbing to the top of an oak tree when he was only three years old. Oak loves to read and write. He has written a number of books about fascinating, terrible, and gruesome events from the distant past. He prefers spending time in the wilderness with his dog, Birchy.

Author: Murray "Oak" Tapeta

Editor: Kathy Middleton

Proofreader: Crystal Sikkens

Design: Samara Parent and Kathy Walsh

Production coordinator: Candice Campbell

IMAGE CREDITS

Alamy: ©Album: p 24-25

Shutterstock: ©Shan_shan: front cover and title page (main image) ©Fedor Selivanov: front cover and title page (bottom); ©Efired: p 4-5, 18-19; ©Mohammed_Al_Ali, p 6 (bottom right); ©Claudine Van Massenhove: p 9 (bottom right); ©Tatiana_kashko_photo: p 10-11; ©Igor Pavluzhenkov: p 14-15; ©canghai76: p 16-17; ©Natali Glado: p 20 (top left); ©Kiev.Victor: p 20-21; ©Hung Chung Chih: p 22-23; ©posztos: p 23 (bottom right); ©PixHound: p 24 (top left), p 25 (bottom left); ©toiletroom: p 26 (bottom left); © DnDavis: p 26-27

Wikimedia Commons: ©Bairuilong: p 15 (bottom right); ©edward stojakovic: p 18 (bottom right); Public domain: p 28 (bottom left); ©风二中 Fēng èr zhōng: p 28-29

All other images from Shutterstock

Crabtree Publishing

crabtreebooks.com 800-387-7650

In Canada: We acknowledge the financial support of the Government of Canada through the Canada Book Fund for our publishing activities.

Hardcover 978-1-0398-7282-0
Paperback 978-1-0398-7340-7
Ebook (pdf) 978-1-0398-7395-7
Epub 978-1-0398-7444-2

Published in Canada
Crabtree Publishing
616 Welland Avenue
St. Catharines, Ontario
L2M 5V6

Published in the United States
Crabtree Publishing
347 Fifth Avenue
Suite 1402-145
New York, New York, 10016

Library and Archives Canada Cataloguing in Publication
Available at Library and Archives Canada

Library of Congress Cataloging-in-Publication Data
Available at the Library of Congress

Printed in the U.S.A./CP052026